J
610   cl
SWA
Swanson, Diane
The Doctor and You

The Doctor & You

Visiting

When you visit the doctor, take along a toy "friend." You might see other toys there, too.

Every day you do things that help you stay well: eat, sleep, run around, keep clean and buckle up during car rides. But like everyone else, you need a little extra help now and then. That's why you visit doctors: to get better when you're sick or injured and to keep healthy.

Visiting doctors means taking trips to offices, clinics or hospitals where there are special tools to care for you. The doctors use many of them. Nurses and medical technicians use some, too. The tools that are pictured in this book are common ones. You'll spot many or all of them on your doctor visits — even if the tools don't look exactly like the ones on these pages.

The first time you see a doctor's tools, they can seem strange — even a bit scary — so they might worry you. That's why it's good to read this book with a parent before you visit a doctor. You'll find out how the tools are used and why. You'll discover that most of them won't hurt you at all and that some will — just for a few seconds. But remember: all these tools are there to help you.

You are the person in charge of your body, so you are important to your own care. In this book, you'll read about some of the jobs you'll have at a doctor's office, clinic or hospital. Look for them on pages that say "Your Job." Then try them out on your doctor visits.

Sizing you Up

Think how tiny you were as a baby. You've grown much taller and heavier since then. And you'll be growing for several years more. Doctors check how well you're growing by keeping track of your height and weight. That helps them find out how healthy you are. They use a tool called a scale, but it doesn't look anything like the scale you might have at home.

When you stand on a doctor's scale, a flat rod is lowered to the top of your head. The number it points to is your height.

Two metal weights are slid along a double bar at the top of the scale until the bar is balanced. That shows your weight.

Does the Scale Hurt You?

No. The rod presses only lightly on the top of your head.

Your Job

Take off your shoes. Stand straight and tall with both feet flat on the scale. It jiggles easily, so try to stay still.

Set your toy "friend" aside for this job so it doesn't make you seem heavier than you are.

L ike the TV, fridge or lights in your house, your body uses electricity to work. Small amounts flow inside you along "wires" called nerves. They connect your brain with other parts of your body and make your muscles move. When you think about wiggling your toes or scrunching your nose, you can. Try it.

Some nerves link directly with other nerves. If one sends a signal to another—without travelling first through your brain—it can make a muscle jump without you thinking about it. That action is called a reflex.

Doctors can find out how well your nerves and muscles are working by testing the reflex in your knee — or elbow or ankle. They use a tool called a reflex hammer. It has a small rubber head — **not** at all like the hammers that people use to pound nails. When a reflex hammer taps your leg just below the knee, one nerve signals another directly. Then your leg jerks up on its own.

Does the Reflex Hammer Hurt You?

No. Try tapping your leg just below the knee, using the knuckles on your fist. A reflex hammer feels a bit like that.

Your Job

Let your leg hang l-o-o-s-e, like a cooked spaghetti noodle. Watch it swing suddenly when your knee is tapped. Neat!

Reflex hammers come in different shapes. Compare the one by the patient with the one in the doctor's hand.

In your mouth

Tongue Depressor or Swab Hurt You?

No, but they might make you feel like gagging for a few seconds.

Ever had a sore throat that hurts when you swallow? That can be a sign that you're sick. Doctors check your throat by looking as far down it as they can. They shine a bright light in your mouth, but your tongue — which is almost solid muscle — usually gets in the way. That's why doctors use a tool called a tongue depressor to help you hold it in place. The depressor looks — and feels — like a fat Popsicle stick.

Doctors may need a sample of the germs that are making you sick. They gently rub your throat with a swab — a thin stick with soft cotton on the tip. Then they put the germs in a tube for testing later. Learning what germs you have in your throat helps doctors decide what kind of help you need.

Open your mouth wide. Say, "Ahhh!" That helps the doctor see into your throat. It can also help keep you from gagging.

Look for the swab and tube used to gather throat germs. You may ask for an extra tongue depressor to take home.

Hot Stuff

Armpit thermometer

Ear thermometer

Do Thermometers Hurt You?

No, but they can feel a bit cold at first.

When it's hot, you wear cool clothes and head for the shade. On cold days, you pull on a sweater or a jacket. That's because temperatures outside your body go up and down, unlike the temperature inside you. It holds steady — unless illnesses or infections make it rise. Then we say you have a "fever."

Doctors check your fever by seeing how high your temperature is. They use a tool called a thermometer that measures the heat inside your body.

Thermometers come in different shapes and sizes. Many of the ones that doctors use are electronic, and they work much faster than glass thermometers. Some go under your armpit or in your mouth; others are placed just inside your ear. Usually they beep when they've finished measuring the heat inside your body, and numbers appear to show what your temperature is.

When there's a thermometer under your armpit, snuggle your arm against your body. If there's one in your mouth, hold it still under your tongue and close your mouth around it. If a thermometer is going in your ear, just hold steady for a second or two.

Using an ear thermometer is the fastest way to check your temperature.

If you roll up your sleeve, the doctor can place the armpit thermometer right against your skin.

Eyeing Your Health

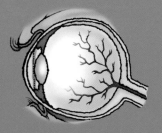

Vessels in your eye

Ophthalmoscope

Does the Ophthalmoscope Hurt You?

No. It doesn't even touch your eye.

Narrow tubes called vessels carry blood around your whole body — and that's a very good thing! Blood delivers oxygen and nutrients from food to every part of you, helping you grow well and stay healthy. It also takes away wastes — things your body parts don't need.

If you make a fist, you can spot some bluish-colored vessels just under the skin on the back of your hand. They may be even easier to find on your parents' hands. But the only place anyone can see blood vessels very clearly is inside an eye.

Doctors check your general health by looking at the vessels in the back of your eyeball. They use a tool called an ophthalmoscope (off-THAL-muh-scope). It has a strong light and a magnifying lens that makes things look bigger than they really are. Doctors put one end of this tool close to your eye and peek through the other end.

Hold your head steady and your eyes open. Look at whatever the doctor asks you to.

The ophthalmoscope lights up your eye and makes it seem larger so the doctor can see the blood vessels inside.

Peer in an Ear

Otoscope

Does the Otoscope Hurt You?

No. Usually it just tickles, and it might feel cold. But if your ear is already sore, anything that touches it can make you feel uncomfortable. Hang in. The otoscope is in your ear for less than a minute.

I t's easy to see in your outer ear. That's the fleshy scoop that picks up all the sounds you hear. But as these sounds travel on inside your head, they enter your middle ear — which is not nearly as easy to see. It's cramped and dark in there.

Doctors check your middle ear to see how healthy it is. If you have an earache, they try to find what's causing it. They use a tool called an otoscope (OAT-uh-scope). It contains a bright light and a magnifying lens, just like the ophthalmoscope that's used to look in your eyes. Some doctors can attach special parts to an ophthalmoscope and — BINGO! — they've got an otoscope. They put one end of it in your ear and peek through the other end.

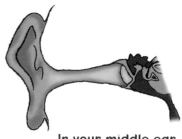

In your middle ear

Hold your head the way you're shown, and try to keep it steady.

An otoscope makes the tiny parts in your middle ear easier to see.

Listening to Lub-Dups

O f all your muscles, your heart is one of the most important. And it's very hard-working. Day and night, year after year, it pumps the blood that flows through the vessels in your body.

Doctors check your heart by listening to it beat. They use a tool called a stethoscope that makes the heartbeats louder and easier to hear. The small round part of the stethoscope is placed on your chest close to your heart.

The noise — which sounds like lub-dup, lub-dup, lub-dup — travels through the hollow tubes of the stethoscope to the doctor's ears. There, it sounds like this: **Lub-Dup, Lub-Dup, Lub-Dup**. Doctors can also use a stethoscope to hear other body sounds: your intestines gurgling, your blood swishing and your lungs breathing.

Does the Stethoscope Hurt You?

No, but it might feel cold against your skin.

Breathe normally — unless you're asked to breathe deeply or to hold your breath. Avoid talking because the noise makes your chest quiver and sounds **really loud** through a stethoscope.

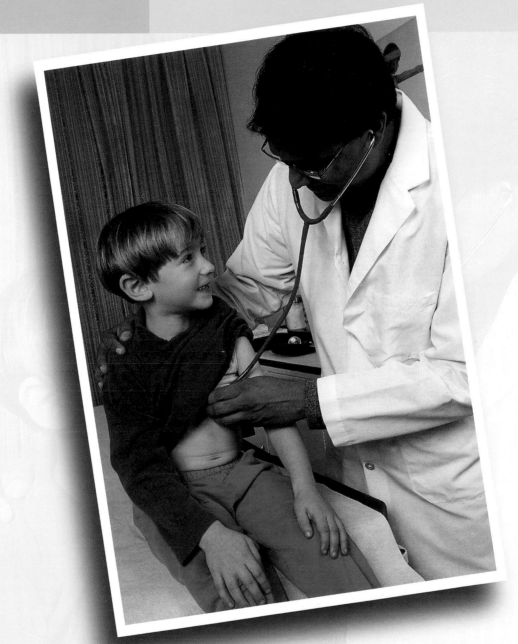

Put your ear on a chest and you can hear heartbeats, but a doctor can hear them better through a stethoscope.

17

Hugs that Help

Doctors check to see how well your heart is pumping blood around your body. They use a tool that you can call a "hug machine." There are different kinds, all with cuffs that wrap around your arm. Sometimes you see hug machines in drugstores, too.

Doctors pump air into the cuffs by squeezing a rubber bulb or by pushing a beeping button on an electronic hug machine. This makes the cuff tighten and — for a few seconds — stops the blood from moving through a vessel in your arm. As soon as the cuff is loosened, the blood starts flowing again. Then doctors read the numbers that light up on electronic machines (you'll hear a beep). With squeeze-bulb machines, doctors use a stethoscope to listen to the sound your blood makes as it starts moving again, and they read numbers from a gauge — part of the hug machine.

Does the Hug Machine Hurt You?

No. The cuff around your arm just feels tight for a moment.

Your Job

Act normally — and smile.
You're being hugged!

Doctors push a button or squeeze a bulb to pump up the cuff of a hug machine. Then they watch the numbers on the electronic machine (left) or the gauge (above).

A Lot in a Little

Testing a few drops of blood can tell doctors a lot. It helps them figure out whether or not you have an infection that's making you sick. Then they can decide how to treat you.

Getting a few drops of blood takes just a minute or two. Medical technicians clean one of your fingertips with a small cloth — an alcohol swab. Next, they squeeze the fingertip slightly and poke it with a tiny tool called a lancet. A bit of blood drips into a small tube. The drops will be tested later, but your part is done. You get a bandage for your finger.

Does the Alcohol Swab or the Lancet Hurt You?

The swab is cold and smells weird, but it doesn't hurt. The poke from the lancet feels like a pinprick — but it's over before you know it.

Your Job

If you want to, use your free hand to hold someone else's hand or a favorite toy. Count — one, two, three — then blow out when you feel the poke.

A quick wipe with an alcohol swab and your fingertip is clean.

Find the little green lancet. It pokes your fingertip so a bit of blood can drip into a tube.

A Little Bit More

Does the Elastic Strip or the Syringe Hurt You?

No. The elastic strip just feels tight. If special cream was used to make your arm numb, the syringe shouldn't hurt at all. The feeling in that numb spot will return in a few hours. If no cream was used, the syringe hurts about as much as a hard pinch.

To discover what's making you sick, doctors might ask medical technicians to test your blood in several ways. Then they need more than a few drops. The technicians at some offices, clinics and hospitals put a glob of special cream on your arm and cover that glob with a clear bandage. After about an hour, the cream makes the spot numb — you won't have any feeling there for a while.

Next, the technicians tie an elastic strip around your arm so your blood vessels are easier to see. They clean the numb area with an alcohol swab. Then they use a hollow needle on a tool called a syringe to draw blood from a vessel in your arm.

When it's over, you end up with a bandage on the spot where the needle was. Don't worry: blood won't keep leaking out, and your body soon makes more blood to replace what was removed.

You might be asked to make a fist to help the doctor find your blood vessels. If you'd rather not watch the syringe, close your eyes and picture a favorite toy, animal or friend. If your arm isn't numb, use your free hand to hold onto someone's hand or a favorite toy, if you like. Count — one, two, three — then blow out when you feel the needle.

A special kind of cream makes your arm so numb (above) that you shouldn't feel a syringe used to draw blood (left).

23

On Guard

What's better than getting well fast? Not getting sick in the first place. Doctors can give you something called vaccines that keep you from getting certain kinds of diseases, such as measles and mumps. You probably had your first vaccine when you were just a baby.

A syringe—like the one that draws blood for testing—delivers some vaccines. Doctors clean a spot on your arm with an alcohol swab. Then they put the tip of the needle just under the skin. The vaccine flows out through the hollow needle and into your arm.

Does the Syringe Hurt You?

What you feel hurts about as much as a hard pinch. The whole thing is over in a blink, but the part of your arm where you felt the needle may be sore for a couple of days. Remember: this small hurt can help you avoid getting some serious diseases later.

With your free hand, hold onto someone else's hand or a favorite toy, if you want. Count — one, two, three — then blow out when you feel the needle. If you don't want to watch, close your eyes and picture something you really like… a juicy apple, a leaping whale…

Getting a vaccine can help keep you well — even if it hurts a bit.

X-ray picture of a
broken leg bone

Does the X-Ray Machine Hurt You?

No. You feel nothing.

I
f you break a bone, doctors need to see just where that bone is broken. They send you to a special room to get pictures of the bone, using a tool called an X-ray machine. It's a big camera that photographs your insides, instead of your outsides. But it can't "see" any of your thoughts, feelings or secrets.

Bones and teeth — even rings or pebbles that people might accidentally swallow — are easiest to photograph. Sometimes X-ray machines also get pictures of soft parts, such as your stomach, especially if you first swallow a medicine that helps your stomach show up.

In an X-ray room, someone shows you how to stand, sit or lie back for the photo. You may be placed on a special kind of bed that can move up and down. If your parents go into the room with you, they're given strange-looking coats to wear. The coats are made of the same material as a little blanket that's put across your lap.

The X-ray camera makes funny noises as it's moved around. It ends up close to the part of you that's being photographed. You may hear more odd noises when the X-ray photos are taken.

Your Job

Stay still so the X-ray machine can get clear pictures. Say "cheese," if you like, even though your smile won't show up on the photos.

Find the photo plate beneath this patient's leg. The X-ray photo of her broken bone will show up there.

Setting You Straight

A broken bone in your leg or arm soon starts to heal. So it's important to make sure that the broken parts stay in the right place. That helps your bone grow back into the same shape it was before it was broken.

Doctors use a tool called a cast — a hard "tube" made of fiberglass or plaster. When it's first formed around your leg or arm, it's quite soft, but a fiberglass cast hardens almost right away. A plaster cast can take a day to harden completely. Neither kind of cast touches your skin. It goes on over soft, fluffy material that's placed gently around your leg or arm.

How long you wear a cast depends on how much time your bone needs to mend. Fiberglass casts are put on legs and arms that need support for a longer time. They're tougher than plaster casts.

When it's time to take off a cast, a special machine cuts through it. The machine whirs like a saw, but it has no blade — so you're not in any danger. Then pliers are used to remove the cast.

Does Getting the Cast On — or Off — Hurt You?

A broken leg or arm is sore, so getting a cast on hurts a bit. The cast feels warm at first, but it cools as it dries. Taking a cast off doesn't hurt at all, but the noise can be surprising.

Hold your leg or arm the way you're shown. Keep steady when the cast is going on or coming off. Breathe deeply to help you relax.

Plaster casts, such as the one on this patient's arm, are chalky white.

Fiberglass casts, such as this leg cast, can be made in many colors — even in candy cane stripes.

Points for Parents

- ▶ Share this book with your children before they visit a doctor. It can reduce anxiety by helping them become familiar with the tools and treatments that doctors use.
- ▶ Read the book out loud and study the pictures with your children. Encourage them to ask questions and discuss what they hear and see.
- ▶ Be open and honest in answering your children's questions and addressing their fears, but stress the positive value of visiting a doctor.
- ▶ Ask your children how well they think the patients in the photos are doing their "jobs."
- ▶ Have your children find the toys that appear with these patients. Suggest they choose a "comfort toy" of their own to bring with them on their visits to a doctor.
- ▶ If possible, provide toy doctor or nurse kits and encourage your children to play with them. Such play can help overcome fears and make children feel more comfortable with real medical tools and treatments.
- ▶ Try to observe your children while they're playing doctor or nurse. They may display fears that they have been reluctant to talk about. Then you can initiate discussions, offer reassurance and clarify any misconceptions.
- ▶ Some children wrongly believe that medical treatments are punishments for bad behavior. Watch for signs of such attitudes and reassure your children that treatments are solely about getting better and staying well.
- ▶ Plan a simple — but fun — event that your children can anticipate and enjoy following a visit to the doctor. It can help to end the day on a high note.

After a visit to the doctor

- ▶ Praise your children for trying to do their special "job" during each procedure or treatment — even if they didn't do it very well. Show appreciation for whatever effort they made, and encourage them to try harder next time.
- ▶ Reread this book with your children. Discuss how their doctor's visit and the tools used were similar and how they were different from the ones you read about. Invite your children to ask questions about their visit.
- ▶ Encourage your children to keep playing doctor and nurse. As before, watch for signs of fears or concerns and try to address them.

Index

Annick Press Ltd.

Cataloging in Publication Data

Swanson, Diane, 1944–
          The doctor and you

ISBN 1-55037-673-X (bound)   ISBN 1-55037-672-1(pbk.)

1. Medicine – Juvenile literature. 2. Physicians – Juvenile literature.
I. Title.

R130.5.S92 2001   j610   C00-932608-1

Editing by Elizabeth McLean
Design by Irvin Cheung & Lisa Ma / iCheung Design
Cover photograph by Jo-Ann Richards
All interior photographs by Jo-Ann Richards except pages 5, 9, 17, 19 (top), which are by Warren Hale
The text was typeset in ITC Century Book and Keedy Sans

Acknowledgments

For their help in producing this book, I am extremely grateful to the staff of the Victoria General Hospital — especially Child Life specialist Pat Hook, who acted as technical consultant for the project — and also William Blair, Susanne Bourgh, Deb Davis, Sandy Jhuti, Lianne Peterson, Samaya Rayne and Richard Thomas, to the St. Clair–Dufferin Medical Centre in Toronto and to Dr. Ruth Campling of North Vancouver.

Many thanks go to Michael and Gwyn Barrodale, Alexander and William Ge, Hilevy and Carmen Mejia, Maria Osman and Habiba Hassan, as well as students from Charlton Public School who posed in the photographs.

Special assistance provided by Eileen Pangman, Diane Silvey, Wayne Swanson and Susan Wilks is greatly appreciated.

Published in the U.S.A. by
Annick Press (U.S.) Ltd.

Distributed in Canada by
Firefly Books Ltd.
3680 Victoria Park Avenue
Willowdale, ON
M2H 3K1

Distributed in the U.S.A. by
Firefly Books (U.S.) Inc.
P.O. Box 1338
Ellicott Station
Buffalo, NY 14205

Printed and bound in Canada by Kromar Printing Ltd.

Visit our website at www.annickpress.com